MAX on life
cd-book :: study

Finding Strength
for Your
Struggles

4 Interactive Bible Studies
for Individuals or Small Groups

MAX LUCADO

THOMAS NELSON PUBLISHERS

CONTENTS

HOW TO USE
THIS STUDY GUIDE

Congratulations! You are making God's Word a priority. These moments of reflection will change you forever. Here are a few suggestions for you to get the most out of your individual study.

1

As you begin each study, pray that God will speak to you through His Word.

2

Read the overview to each study, then listen to the audio segment, taking notes on the worksheet provided.

3

Following the audio segment, respond to the personal Bible study and reflection questions. These questions are designed to take you deeper into God's Word and help you focus on God and on the theme of the study.

4

There are three types of questions used in the study. *Observation* questions focus on the basic facts: who, what, when, where, and how. *Interpretation* questions delve into the meaning of the passage. *Application* questions help you get practical: discovering the implications of the text for growing in Christ. These three keys will help you unlock the treasures of Scripture.

5

Write your answers to the questions in the spaces provided or in a personal journal. Writing brings clarity and deeper understanding of yourself and of God's Word.

6

Keep a Bible dictionary handy. Use it to look up any unfamiliar words, names, or places.

7

Have fun! Studying God's Word can bring tremendous rewards to your life. Allow the Holy Spirit to illuminate your mind to the amazing applications each study can have in your daily life. ■

INTRODUCTION

FINDING STRENGTH
FOR YOUR STRUGGLES

Imagine yourself in a jungle. A dense jungle. A dark jungle. Your friends convinced you it was time for a once-in-a-lifetime trip, and here you are. You paid the fare. You crossed the ocean. You hired the guide and joined the group. And you ventured where you had never ventured before—into the thick, strange world of the jungle.

Sound interesting? Let's take it a step farther. You are in the jungle, lost and alone. You paused to lace your boot, and when you looked up, no one was near. You took a chance and went to the right; now you're wondering if the others went to the left. (Or did you go left and they go right?)

For many people, life is—well, life is a jungle. Not a jungle of trees and beasts. Would that it were so simple. Would that our jungles could be cut with a machete or our adversaries trapped in a cage.

But our struggles are more complex. Our jungles are comprised of the thicker thickets of failing health, broken hearts, and empty wallets. Our forests are framed with hospital walls and divorce courts. Our predators are our creditors, and the brush that surrounds us is the rush that exhausts us.

Is your life a jungle? Confusing? Difficult to maneuver? Scary? God has provided you with all you need to make it through the jungle of life. ■

*Salvation is not
turning over a new leaf
but receiving a new life.*

AUTHOR UNKNOWN

LESSON ONE:

A SECOND CHANCE AT LIFE

*Because of the Lord's great love we are
not consumed, for his compassions never
fail. They are new every morning;
great is your faithfulness.*

LAMENTATIONS 3:22–23 NIV

OVERVIEW

It has been a long day. Jerusalem is packed with Passover guests, most of whom clamor for a glimpse of the Teacher. The spring sun is warm. The streets are dry. And the disciples are a long way from home. A splash of cool water would be refreshing.

The disciples enter, one by one, and take their places around the table. On the wall hangs a towel, and on the floor sits a pitcher and a basin. Any one of the disciples could volunteer for the job, but no one does.

After a few moments, Jesus stands and removes His outer garment. He wraps a servant's girdle around His waist, takes up the basin, and kneels before one of the disciples. He unlaces a sandal and gently lifts the foot and places it in the basin, covers it with water, and begins to bathe it. One by one, one grimy foot after another, Jesus works His way down the row.

In Jesus' day the washing of feet was a task reserved not just for servants but for the lowest of servants. Every circle has its pecking order, and the circle of household workers was no exception. The servant at the bottom of the totem pole was expected to be the one on his knees with the towel and basin.

In this case the one with the towel and basin is the King of the universe. Hands that shaped the stars now wash away filth. Fingers that formed mountains now massage toes. And the One before whom all nations will one day kneel now kneels before His disciples. Hours before His own death, Jesus' concern is singular. He wants his disciples to know how much He loves them. More than removing dirt, Jesus is removing doubt.

Jesus knows what will happen to His hands at the crucifixion. Within twenty-four hours they will be pierced and lifeless. Of all the times we'd expect Him to ask for the disciples' attention, this would be one. But He doesn't.

You can be sure Jesus knows the future of these feet He is washing. These twenty-four feet will not spend the next day following their master, defending His cause. These feet will dash for cover at the flash of a Roman sword. Only one pair of feet won't abandon Him in the garden. One disciple won't desert Him at Gethsemane—Judas won't even make it that far! He will abandon Jesus that very night at the table.

I looked for a Bible translation that reads, "Jesus washed all the disciples' feet except the feet of Judas," but I couldn't find one. What a passionate moment when Jesus silently lifts the feet of His betrayer and washes them in the basin! Within hours the feet of Judas, cleansed by the kindness of the one he will betray, will stand in Caiaphas's court.

Behold the gift Jesus gave His followers! He knows what these men are about to do. He knows they are about to perform the vilest act of their lives. By morning they will bury their heads in shame and look down at their feet in disgust. And when they do, He wants them to remember how His knees knelt before them and He washes their feet. He wants them to realize those feet are still clean. "You don't understand now what I am doing, but you will understand later" (John 13:7).

Remarkable. He forgave their sin before they even committed it. He offered mercy before they even sought it. He gave them a second chance.

Do you need a second chance? You've come to the right place. You have a Savior who specializes in second chances. And realizing God's mercy and grace—receiving the second chance He has for you—is the first step toward receiving His strength for your struggles.

PART 1:
FOLLOW-ALONG NOTES

USE THIS WORKSHEET AS YOU LISTEN TO "FINDING STRENGTH FOR YOUR STRUGGLES, PART 1."

- The night that Peter denied Christ was the night that Jesus needed him the most.

- The very thing Peter said he wouldn't do, he did!

- Your story begins and ends with the _____ of Christ.

There's more to your story!

Scene One: The _____
   Matthew 26:31
   It's not necessary to re-crucify Jesus.

Scene Two: Peter's _____
   Matthew 26:33, 35
   Peter should have prayed, not boasted.

Scene Three: The _____
Matthew 26:70, 72, 74
   Three times, Peter tells the people he doesn't know who Jesus is.

But God gives second chances!

PART 2: GOING DEEPER

PERSONAL STUDY AND REFLECTION

If you could you do it all over again, you'd do it differently. You'd be a different person. You'd be more patient. You'd control your tongue. You'd finish what you started. You'd turn the other cheek instead of slapping his. You'd get married first. You wouldn't marry at all. You'd be honest. You'd resist the temptation. You'd run with a different crowd.

But you can't. And as many times as you tell yourself, "What's done is done," what you did can't be undone.

· What major decisions or actions in your own life would you change if you could?

_____

_____

_____

· What dangers are there in rehearsing past personal errors? What benefits
  are there?

  _____

  _____

  _____

  _____

· Have you ever longed for a father who, even though your mistakes were
  written all over the wall, would love you anyway? Have you ever wanted a
  father who cared for you in spite of your failures?

  _____

  _____

  _____

  _____

- What kind of heavenly Father do we have? How has He shown His love and forgiveness to you?

_____

_____

_____

_____

- Read Acts 13:13; Acts 15:36–41; and 2 Timothy 4:11. Describe the failure of John Mark. How serious, in Paul's mind, was this failure?

_____

_____

_____

_____

· What happened in Acts 15:36–41 as a direct result of this failure?

_____

_____

_____

_____

· The text doesn't mention how John Mark felt about this controversy. If you were in his shoes, what might you have felt?

_____

_____

_____

_____

- How does 2 Timothy 4:11 show that Mark's failure was not fatal? What had changed over time?

_____

_____

_____

_____

- What lessons can you learn from the experience of John Mark?

_____

_____

_____

_____

If you have trouble experiencing God's grace and offer of a second chance, it will take time for you to feel free of your guilt. Over the next week, take time to identify those things that keep you from accepting failure as a normal part of life. Here are some things to think through and write down:

- Do you have specific memories of times when you have failed and then been punished?

_____

_____

_____

- How have the significant people in your life affected your view of failure?

_____

_____

_____

- Can you remember times when you have failed and the results were used for good in your life?

_____

_____

_____

_____

_____

God is the God of the second chance! ■

*It's a good thing to have all the props
pulled out from under us occasionally.
It gives us some sense of what is rock
under our feet, and what is sand.*

MADELEINE L'ENGLE

LESSON TWO:

STANDING STRONG IN LIFE'S STORMS

In this world you
will have trouble, but be brave!
I have defeated the world.

JOHN 16:33B

OVERVIEW

There are many examples of Jesus' power and authority, but I want to share with you one of my favorites. Jesus and the disciples are in a boat crossing the Sea of Galilee. A storm arises suddenly, and what was placid becomes violent—monstrous waves rise out of the sea and slap the boat. Mark describes it clearly: "A furious squall came up, and the waves broke over the boat, so that it was nearly swamped" (Mark 4:37 NIV).

It's very important that you get an accurate picture, so I'm going to ask you to imagine yourself in the boat. It's a sturdy vessel but no match for these ten-foot waves. It plunges nose first into the wall of water. The force of the waves dangerously tips the boat until the bow seems to be pointing straight at the sky. And just when you fear flipping over backward, the vessel pitches forward into the valley of another wave. A dozen sets of hands join yours in clutching the mast. All your shipmates have wet heads and wide eyes. You tune your ear for a calming voice, but all you hear are screams and prayers. All of a sudden it hits you—someone is missing. Where is Jesus? He's not at the mast. He's not grabbing the edge, either. Where is He? Then you hear something—a noise . . . a displaced sound . . . like someone is snoring. You turn and look, and there curled in the stern of the boat is Jesus, sleeping!

You don't know whether to be amazed or angry, so you're both. How can He sleep at a time like this? Or as the disciples asked, "Teacher, don't you care if we drown?" (Mark 4:38 NIV).

The very storm that made the disciples panic made Him drowsy. What put fear in their eyes put Him to sleep. The boat was a tomb to the followers and a cradle to Christ. How could He sleep through the storm? Simple—He was in charge of it.

He got up, rebuked the wind and said to the waves, "Quiet! Be still!" Then the wind died down and it was completely calm. He said to his disciples, "Why are you so afraid? Do you still have no faith?" (Mark 4:39–40 NIV)

Incredible. He doesn't chant a mantra or wave a wand. No angels are called; no help is needed. The raging water becomes a stilled sea, instantly. Immediate calm. Not a ripple. Not a drop. Not a gust. In a moment the sea goes from a churning torrent to a peaceful pond. The reaction of the disciples? Read it in verse 41: "They were in absolute awe, staggered. 'Who is this, anyway?' they asked. 'Wind and sea at his beck and call!'" (MSG).

They'd never met a man like this. The waves were His subjects, and the winds were His servants. It's only right that they declared Jesus' authority. And it's only right that we do the same.

PART 1:
FOLLOW-ALONG NOTES

USE THIS WORKSHEET AS YOU LISTEN TO "FINDING STRENGTH FOR YOUR STRUGGLES, PART 2."

- Jesus had to face impossibilities in the busiest day of His life.

- Matthew 14:23: Jesus went up the _____ to pray.

- During the storm, Jesus _____.

- Jesus did not try to do it by Himself—why should you?

- Why do we go through difficult times? Where is God when I hurt?

- If the disciples had the chance to go through the storm again, they would.

- It was through the storm they saw the Savior.

- Matthew 14:32: After the storm, the disciples worshiped Jesus.

- This time they were the ones who were saved.

- Only when God _____ you will you _____ Him.

- When you genuinely ask, He will come.

PART 2:
GOING DEEPER

PERSONAL STUDY AND REFLECTION

God is with you. Knowing that, who is against you? Can death harm you now? Can disease rob your life? Can your purpose be taken or your value diminished? No. Though hell itself may set itself against you, no one can defeat you. You are protected. God is with you.

- How do you tend to react in trying times? (Be honest!)

_____

_____

_____

_____

_____

Read Romans 8:31–39.

- Explain Paul's logic behind his statement in verse 32. Why is this statement so crucial to winning the spiritual battles that we face every day?

_____

_____

_____

_____

- In what ways are the questions of verses 33–35 related? What is their function?

_____

_____

_____

_____

· How can the quotation found in verse 36 actually be an encouragement?
How is it intended to function in this way?

_____

_____

_____

_____

· Does Paul leave anything out of verses 38–39? What does he intend for us
to understand? How does he want these truths to encourage us?

_____

_____

_____

_____

Read Isaiah 49:15–16.

· What question is asked in verse 15? What answer is expected? What comparison is intended with the subsequent statement?

_____

_____

_____

_____

· What metaphor does God use in verse 16? What is His point? What does He want us to believe? Why?

_____

_____

_____

· How can a person be sure that bad times aren't a signal of God's displeasure with him or her?

_____

_____

_____

_____

· What gives Christians confidence as they face struggles or go through hard times?

_____

_____

_____

_____

- In what situations do you need God's conquering power today?

_____

_____

_____

- How can you commit your difficult circumstance to God this week?

_____

_____

_____

- How can you show trust that God will work out your circumstances for good?

_____

_____

_____

*Worry is putting question marks
where God has put periods.*

JOHN R. RICE

LESSON THREE:

TRUSTING MORE, WORRYING LESS

Do not worry about anything,
but pray and ask God
for everything you need,
always giving thanks.

PHILIPPIANS 4:6

OVERVIEW

"When all that is good falls apart,
what can good people do?"
The LORD is in his holy temple;
the LORD sits on his throne in heaven.
Psalm 11:3–4

Isn't David's question ours? When all that is good falls apart, what can good people do? When illness invades, marriages fail, children suffer, and death strikes, what are we to do? How can we find strength in our struggles when the difficulties of life threaten to overcome us?

Curiously, David doesn't answer his question with an answer. He answers it with a declaration: "The LORD is in his holy temple; the LORD sits on his throne in heaven."

His point is unmistakable: God is unaltered by our storms. He is undeterred by our problems. He is not frightened by the things that frighten us. He is in His holy temple. He is on His throne in heaven.

Buildings may fall, careers may crumble, but God does not. Wreckage and rubble have never discouraged Him. God has always turned tragedy into triumph. Did He not do so with Joseph? Look at Joseph in the Egyptian prison. His brothers have sold him out;

Potiphar's wife has turned him in. If ever a world has caved in, Joseph's has.

Or consider Moses, watching flocks in the wilderness. Is this what he intended to do with his life? Hardly. His heart beats with Jewish blood. His passion is to lead the slaves, so why does God have him leading sheep?

And Daniel. What about Daniel? He was among the brightest and best young men of Israel, the equivalent of a West Point cadet or an Ivy Leaguer. But he and his entire generation are being marched out of Jerusalem. The city is destroyed. The Temple is in ruins.

Joseph in prison. Moses in the desert. Daniel in chains. These were dark moments. Who could have seen any good in them? Joseph the prisoner was just one promotion from becoming Joseph the prime minister? Who would have thought that God was giving Moses forty years of wilderness training in the very desert through which he would lead the people? And who could have imagined that Daniel the captive would soon be Daniel the king's counselor?

God does things like that. He did with Joseph, with Moses, and with Daniel. God is still in His temple, still on His throne, and still in control—therefore, there is no reason to fear. Today we will discuss the next step in finding strength for your struggles: relinquishing those struggles to the God who is still on the throne.

PART 1:
FOLLOW-ALONG NOTES

USE THIS WORKSHEET AS YOU LISTEN TO "FINDING STRENGTH FOR YOUR STRUGGLES, PART 3."

- John 6:1–14

- Do you have too many demands and not enough resources?

- The solution was standing right in front of the disciples, and they didn't even know it!

- The Greek word for worry means to _____.

- The German word for worry means to _____.

- Four Steps to Help in Times of Anxiety

1. Carefully _____ your vision (verse 11).
"To whom am I looking?"

2. Gratefully _____ the problem (verse 11).
Jesus thanked God for the bread He did have.

3. Faithfully _____ a step (verses 10, 12).
Jesus let the disciples be part of the solution. Their distrust was overcome by obedience.

4. Openly give God the _____ (verse 14).
All we do is deliver what we've been given.

- Have you really given your problem to Jesus?

PART 2:
GOING DEEPER

PERSONAL STUDY AND REFLECTION

· Our approach to life says a lot about how much we believe God cares for us. Little faith? Little amount of trust? Large faith? Large amount of trust? How do you see yourself? (Check all that apply.)

___ I prefer to be in control of my life at all times.

___ In the big decisions of life, I am willing to take a leap of faith. God won't let me down.

___ God doesn't care about the routine areas of my day. I save my faith for the big stuff.

___ My faith is enough to encompass the seemingly small areas in life where it is tested.

___ I believe what God has said, and that affects how I live out my day.

Read John 6:1–14.

- Why did the crowd of people follow Jesus? (verse 2)

_____

_____

- What question did Jesus ask Philip? Why did He ask this? (verses 5–6)

_____

_____

- What was Andrew's solution? (verses 8–9)

_____

_____

_____

_____

- What miracle did Jesus perform? (verses 10–11)

_____

_____

_____

_____

- How much bread was left over? (verses 12–13)

_____

_____

_____

_____

- Jesus provided miraculously for the people who had come to Him. How and when has God miraculously provided for your needs? Tell the story.

_____

_____

_____

_____

_____

_____

- How does this story help you better understand God's concern for your needs?

_____

_____

· Read the following verses. Then match the verse with what you learn about God's care for you.

A. Psalm 10:14   ___ He always helps in times of trouble.

B. Psalm 34:15   ___ He will make us strong and support us.

C. Psalm 46:1   ___ He listens to our prayers.

D. Isaiah 41:10   ___ He helps us when we feel like orphans.

· Read 1 Peter 5:7. What does this verse instruct you to do with your worries and cares?

_____

_____

· Why should you do this?

_____

_____

- What does it mean, in a practical sense, to "cast your anxieties" on the Lord?

  _____

  _____

- What anxieties are you currently facing?

  _____

  _____

  _____

- How can you turn these difficult situations over to God this week and trust Him to work things out on your behalf?

  _____

  _____

*Most of the important things in the world
have been accomplished by people
who have kept on trying when there seemed
to be no hope at all.*

DALE CARNEGIE

LESSON FOUR:

HOW HURTS BRING HOPE

But those who hope in the Lord will renew their strength. They will soar on wings like eagles; they will run and not grow weary, they will walk and not be faint.

ISAIAH 40:31 NIV

OVERVIEW

It's early dawn on Sunday morning and the sky is dark. Those, in fact, are John's words. "It was still dark . . ." (John 20:1).

It's a dark Sunday morning. It had been dark since Friday.

Two Marys, one the mother of James and Joseph, and the other, Mary Magdalene, leave their pallets and walk out onto the tree-shadowed path. Theirs is a somber path. The morning promises only one encounter, an encounter with a corpse.

Remember, Mary and Mary don't know this is the first Easter. They are not hoping the tomb will be vacant. They aren't discussing what their response will be when they see Jesus. They have absolutely no idea that the grave has been vacated.

There was a time when they dared to dream such dreams. Not now. It's too late for the incredible. The feet that walked on water had been pierced. The hands that healed lepers had been stilled. Noble aspirations had been spiked into Friday's cross. Mary and Mary have come to place warm oils on a cold body and bid farewell to the one man who gave reason to their hopes.

I wonder if halfway to the tomb they sat down and reconsidered. What if they'd looked at each other and shrugged, "What's the use?" What if they had given up?

Whether or not they were tempted to, I'm glad they didn't quit. That would have been tragic. You see, we know something they didn't. We know the Father was watching. Mary and Mary thought they were alone. They weren't. They thought their journey was unnoticed. They were wrong. God knew. He was watching them walk up the mountain. He was measuring their steps. He was smiling at their hearts and thrilled at their devotion. And He had a surprise waiting for them.

"Suddenly, Jesus met them and said, 'Greetings.' The women came up to him, took hold of his feet, and worshiped him. Then Jesus said to them, 'Don't be afraid. Go and tell my followers to go on to Galilee, and they will see me there'" (Matthew 28:9–10).

The God of surprises strikes again. It's as if He said, "I can't wait any longer. They came this far to see Me; I'm going to drop in on them."

God does that for the faithful. Just when the womb gets too old for babies, Sarai gets pregnant. Just when the failure is too great for grace, David is pardoned. And just when the road is too dark for Mary and Mary, the angel glows and the Savior shows and the two women will never be the same.

Is the trail dark? Don't sit.

Is the road long? Don't stop.

Is the night black? Don't quit.

God is watching. For all you know, right at this moment, He may be telling the angel to move the stone.

Are there dreams that you are afraid to dream? God wants to awaken your hope and breathe resurrection life into your heart. And when you pursue the final step in finding strength for your struggles, He will awaken your dreams and turn your hurts into hope.

PART 1:
FOLLOW-ALONG NOTES

USE THIS WORKSHEET AS YOU LISTEN TO FINDING STRENGTH FOR YOUR STRUGGLES, PART 4."

- John 4: The Healing of the Royal Official's Son

- The centurion had a desperate faith.

- All of us are desperate. We are all in the same situation.

- Does God hear our prayers? Yes, because He is our _____.

- We shouldn't live in a state of _____; we should live in a state of _____.

- What's your role? To quit _____ and start _____.

- God can see more than we can—and His methods are best.

- Is this man's journey like yours?

PART 2:
GOING DEEPER

PERSONAL STUDY AND REFLECTION

· As a saying goes, people can live without many things, but they cannot live without hope. There is no hope without God. Check out the following Bible verses and match the verse with the hope that we have in God.

A. Psalm 33:18   ___We have hope in God's Word.

B. Psalm 42:11   ___ Hope in Him secures our future.

C. Psalm 62:5   ___ Hope in Him chases away our sadness.

D. Psalm 119:74   ___ We have hope in His love.

E. Proverbs 23:18   ___ We can rest in His hope.

- Read John 4:46–54.

- What had Jesus previously done in Cana? (verse 46). How might this have affected the royal official's faith?

  _____

  _____

- What was Jesus' response to the man? (verse 48)

  _____

  _____

- How did the man demonstrate hope in Jesus' promise of healing? (verse 50)

  _____

  _____

  _____

  _____

- Why is it sometimes hard to "take Jesus at His word"? What difference could such hope make in your circumstances?

  _____

  _____

- Jesus wants you to be overwhelmed with hope! Read Romans 15:13 and fill in the blanks concerning Paul's prayer that our hope would overflow.

- I pray that the _____ who gives _____ will fill you with much _____ and _____ while you trust in him. Then your _____ will overflow by the _____ _____ of the _____ Spirit.

- Romans 5:5 also speaks of God's hope. What will this hope never do?

  _____

  _____

- Why?

  _____

  _____

· What would it mean to you to face your circumstances knowing that your hope in God would never be disappointed?

_____

_____

_____

_____

· How would your attitude or actions change?

_____

_____

_____

_____

_____ ■

PROMISES FROM
FINDING STRENGTH
FOR YOUR STRUGGLES

Savor the following promises that God offers us in the midst of our difficult circumstances. One way that you can carry the message of this study with you everywhere in your heart is through the lost art of memorization. Select a few of the verses below to commit to memory.

"When all that is good falls apart, what can good people do?"
The Lord is in his holy temple; the Lord sits on his throne in heaven.

PSALM 11:3–4

"I know what I am planning for you," says the Lord. "I have good plans
for you, not plans to hurt you. I will give you hope and a good future."

JEREMIAH 29:11B

Do not worry about anything, but pray and ask God for everything you
need, always giving thanks.

PHILIPPIANS 4:6

If God is with us, no one can defeat us.

ROMANS 8:31B

The Lord answers, "Can a woman forget the baby she nurses?
Can she feel no kindness for the child to which she gave birth?
Even if she could forget her children, I will not forget you.
See, I have written your name on my hand."

ISAIAH 49:15–16A

Yes, I am sure that neither death, nor life, nor angels, nor ruling spirits,
nothing now, nothing in the future, no powers, nothing above us, nothing
below us, nor anything else in the whole world will ever be able to separate
us from the love of God that is in Christ Jesus our Lord.

ROMANS 8:38–39

I pray that the God who gives hope will fill you with much joy and
peace while you trust in him. Then your hope will overflow by the
power of the Holy Spirit.

ROMANS 15:13 ■

SUGGESTIONS FOR MEMBERS OF A GROUP STUDY

The Bible says that we should not forsake the assembling of ourselves together (see Hebrews 10:25). A small-group Bible study is one of the best ways to grow in your faith. As you meet together with other people, you will discover new truths about God's Word and challenge one another to greater levels of faith. The following are suggestions for you to get the most out of a small-group study of this material.

1. Come to the study prepared. Follow the suggestions for individual study mentioned previously. You will find that careful preparation will greatly enrich your time spent in group discussion.

2. Be willing to participate in the discussion. The leader of your group will not be lecturing. Instead, he or she will be encouraging the members of the group to discuss what they have learned. The leader will be asking the questions that are found in this guide.

3. Stick to the topic being discussed.

4. Be sensitive to the other members of the group. Listen attentively when they describe what they have learned. You may be surprised by their insights! Many questions do not have "right" answers, particularly questions that aim at meaning or application. Instead the questions push us to explore the passage more thoroughly.

5. When possible, link what you say to the comments of others. Also be affirming whenever you can. This will encourage some of the more hesitant members of the group to participate.

6. Expect God to teach you through the passage being discussed and through the other members of the group. Pray that you will have an enjoyable and profitable time together, but also that as a result of this study, you will find ways that you can take action individually and/or as a group.

7. Remember that anything said in the group is considered confidential and should not be discussed outside the group unless specific permission is given to do so. ■

LEADER'S GUIDE

1. Begin the session with prayer. Ask God to be with you as you begin to study His Word together.

2. Play the audio segment of the CD entitled "Finding Strength for Your Struggles, Part 1." Encourage group members to take notes in the section of their study guide entitled "Follow-Along Notes."

3. Begin group discussion by asking the following questions. Allow each group member ample time to answer, if they desire to do so.

   - When have you most needed a second chance? Were you given one? Why or why not? How did this affect you?

   - Why do you think people reject God's offer of a second chance? Why do people continue to feel guilty after asking for God's forgiveness for what they have done?

- Read Psalm 32:1–2. What do these verses tell you about God's willingness to offer a second chance?

4. Remind everyone to complete the "Going Deeper: Personal Study and Reflection" section for lesson two before the next group session.

5. Be sure to close in prayer. Invite the group participants to share prayer requests with the group and encourage them to pray for one another.

LESSON TWO: STANDING STRONG IN LIFE'S STORMS

1. Begin the session with prayer. Ask God to be with you as you begin to study His Word together.

2. Play the audio segment of the CD entitled "Finding Strength for Your Struggles, Part 2." Encourage group members to take notes in the section of their study guide entitled "Follow-Along Notes."

3. Begin group discussion by asking the following questions. Allow each group member ample time to answer, if they desire to do so.

   • How do you tend to react in trying times? Do you ever feel that God is not as great as you say He is? Explain.

   • What is it about "life's storms" that often brings people to Jesus?

   • When are you most likely to fear that God is *not* with you or able to help you in the struggles that you face? How do you respond to these instances?

- How can you begin to turn over your most difficult circumstances to the Lord and trust in God to help you overcome the obstacles you are facing today?

4. Remind everyone to complete the "Going Deeper: Personal Study and Reflection" section for lesson three before the next group session.

5. Be sure to close in prayer. Invite the group participants to share prayer requests with the group and encourage them to pray for one another.

LESSON THREE: TRUSTING MORE, WORRYING LESS

1. Begin the session with prayer. Ask God to be with you as you begin to study His Word together.

2. Play the audio segment of the CD entitled "Finding Strength for Your Struggles, Part 3." Encourage group members to take notes in the section of their study guide entitled "Follow-Along Notes."

3. Begin group discussion by asking the following questions. Allow each group member ample time to answer, if they desire to do so.

   • What is the most difficult situation in which you have ever found yourself? How did God bring you through it?

   • With what circumstances do you have the most difficulty trusting God? Why?

   • How do you usually handle worry and stress? What are your strategies?

- Sometimes holding on to worry indicates a fear of giving up control. How can giving up this control lead to a greater trust in God? How is this true in your own life?

4. Remind everyone to complete the "Going Deeper: Personal Study and Reflection" section for lesson four before the next group session.

5. Be sure to close in prayer. Invite the group participants to share prayer requests with the group and encourage them to pray for one another.

LESSON FOUR: HOW HURTS BRING HOPE

1. Begin the session with prayer. Ask God to be with you as you begin to study His Word together.

2. Play the audio segment of the CD entitled "Finding Strength for Your Struggles, Part 4." Encourage group members to take notes in the section of their study guide entitled "Follow-Along Notes."

3. Begin group discussion by asking the following questions. Allow each group member ample time to answer, if they desire to do so.

   • Complete this sentence any way you'd like: "I hope that . . ."

   • The Bible says that the royal official took Jesus at His word. What are some things in which people believe that they either haven't seen or can't see?

   • To what negative things to people often turn in times of sorrow or suffering? To what positive things might they turn instead?

   • What impact would a miraculous event make in your life? Do you believe such an event could happen? Why or why not?

4. Be sure to close in prayer. Invite the group participants to share prayer requests with the group and encourage them to pray for one another. ■

MAX LUCADO'S

MAX on life

S E R I E S

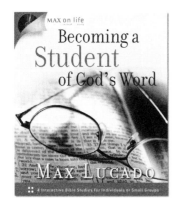

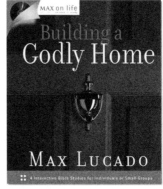

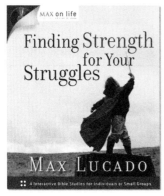

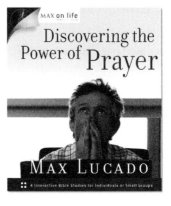

AVAILABLE WHEREVER BOOKS ARE SOLD.